LOVE EVER AFTER

SELECTED SONNETS

1971-2024

LOVE EVER AFTER

SELECTED SONNETS

1971-2024

ARTURO LEWIS JARAMILLO

SUNSTONE PRESS
SANTA FE

Sunstone books may be purchased for educational, business, or sales promotional use.
For information please write: Special Markets Department, Sunstone Press,
P.O. Box 2321, Santa Fe, New Mexico 87504-2321.
Printed on acid-free paper
∞

LIBRARY OF CONGRESS CATALOGING IN PUBLICATION DATA

(ON FILE)

———————————————

WWW.SUNSTONEPRESS.COM
SUNSTONE PRESS / POST OFFICE BOX 2321 / SANTA FE, NM 87504-2321 /USA
(505) 988-4418

DEDICATION

This collection of sonnets is dedicated to Jayne, my wife and partner in life, for her constant reminder that love is many special things comforting to the mind and soul. It is a magical journey, Jayne.

NOTE FROM THE AUTHOR

This book is a work of fiction, a composite of the author's imagination and his idealized recollection of people and events he encountered over the last fifty-six years. The names and personalities of the characters have been changed. The subjects, descriptions, events, occurrences and contributions in the book have been recreated for dramatic, narrative and other literary purposes. The actions, perspectives and opinions expressed in this book are those of literary characters only; they do not necessarily reflect or represent the actions, views or opinions held by the author or by any individual upon whom the literary characters may be based.

CONTENTS

FOREWORD

Composing a sonnet is a challenging exercise in poetic structure and expression. The word "sonnet" is taken from the Italian *sonetto*, "a little sound or song."[1] The sonnets selected for this book are written in Shakespearean form, comprised of three quatrains and a concluding couplet.[2] The imposing rhyme scheme and harmonic flow of this poetic form require the poet to express ideas, images and sentiments concisely, with a consistent melodic quality. Sonnets are beautifully suited for conveying impressions or messages about romance, hope, commitment, nostalgia and passion, themes I often write about in my poetry. With limited words and/or syllables with which to work, symbolism, metaphors and other figurative expressions are typically used to convey intricate concepts and imagery. Interpretation is likewise an important tool in composing and reading sonnets. Looking beyond the express words and phrases of a sonnet searching for deeper meaning can reveal layers of emotion, sentiment or nuances about a theme or story hidden between the lines.

The backstory of the sonnets comprising this book has been described in two previous anthologies of poetry also written by me and published by Sunstone Press.[3] The original book, *Conversations with Quijóte* (2019), is set in 1968, when I began writing poetry as a freshman in college. The idea was to preserve special memories of the people and events that shaped my beliefs about life and romance during the "love generation," by creating images in prose and rhyme about those passionate and chaotic years.[4] That narrative evolved over the next fifty years in the second book, *Impressions Through a Timeworn Lens* (2024). *Impressions* is a retrospective that reimagines the experiences of the love generation and reexamines, with a more seasoned perspective, the idealism and realism that inspired the original book.[5]

Somewhere along this literary journey I began to understand that the sonnets I had composed require no backstory. They stand discretely on their own by their content, setting and form and should be presented separately. The title, verses and rhymes combine to fashion distinctive messages, ideas and a panoply of emotions for readers to interpret and apply to their own sensibilities. That is my impression of the poetic mission. I offer these sonnets as representations of youthful romance, endless love lost and won and a walk through the seasons of life wondering what it all meant. I hope you enjoy reading these sonnets as much as I enjoyed composing them.

Arturo Lewis Jaramillo

Sonnet I

At Fortune's Helm[6]

The falling skies with endless night combine

As tide and time tear down the last few men.

The stars above recede, then misalign;

Unwilling to renew our love again.

And what of you and I, my only dream?

A time ago we shared a love divine.

Will memories continue love's regime;

Or shall, with hope's demise, our love resign?

I know not if the special love we knew

Shall ever be rekindled in the end.

I'm certain time shall hope and trust subdue;

The rest, but god or fortune may extend.

We've shared a love that time cannot erase.

Our romance shall eternity embrace.

February 10, 1971

SONNET II

Redemption

Forlorn, the years misspent in dark despair;

Yet, not a moment lived without your dream.

To join again our lips and love declare

Shall soon my search for endless love redeem.

From pen to prose I've schemed for your return,

Still longing for your comforting embrace.

We meet in shadows, hopeful to discern

If love renewed shall doubtful hearts replace.

You smile the same, though much of you has changed;

The shifting moods, your sorrow soon to tears.

We kiss; make love; promises are exchanged;

And then a favored line to ease your fears:

"I'll hold you tight and savor every day,

Rejecting Frost, that 'nothing gold can stay.'"[7]

February 14, 1971

SONNET III

The March Canticle

You stir as sunrise scatters the morning frost,
A sign that winter's reign has run its course.
As springtime looms, the season our lives crossed,
You rise and shine and lend the rumors force.

Upon this stage, a play; our lives rehearsed;
Left in your wake, my love for you restrained.
Three years now passed; my destiny reversed
As you return for reasons unexplained.

The renaissance of spring renews our trust.
In verdant fields our love and hope abound.
Fate separates the fair from the unjust;
An endless love once lost has now been found?

March, oh myth, my endless love confirmed;
This grateful man accepts her heart returned.

March 2, 1971

SONNET IV

Eid Mar

The Ides and thee three long years passed approach
As we join arms and lay in sweet repose.
Distressed with me, the knight[8] my thoughts reproach
That I did not our love-renewed disclose.

As Caesar feared the Ides, the knight, too, fears.
Will Brutus slay his fame or our affair?
Disheartened with my choice, the knight in tears;
The higher road my love and I will share.

The Ides have blessed my heart with epic charm.
Bright eyes as clear as skies for gifts it bore.
Her lavish kiss I've failed to disarm
And I shall be her captive evermore.

Beware the perplexities of the Ides,
Where Caesar's death with Linda's love collides.

March 7, 1971

SONNET V

March Elegy

Forlorn, my prophecies past; most, ill-conceived.
But as I write, the best may yet come true.
Your love was mine to lose, the knight perceived;
Yet, endless love endures, though overdue.

The year ahead, unknown; our challenge grand,
For few believe our love is sound or true.
I'll not presume what fate may soon demand,
For fate has not been kind to me or you.

So March sixteenth again has come our way.
We met, conversed; a new romance defined.
You're in my arms again and vow to stay,
And never have our stars been so aligned.

Though doubtful our love did once appear,
The promise from your kiss seems so sincere.

March 31, 1971

SONNET VI

To Keep

Our comfort grows, a love affair by night
Replete with pledges far beyond romance.
Our hopes and dreams, through whispers, my delight,
Assure our fragile love shall have its chance.

Your fear of "breaking out," what parents say,
Our union "was the cause of your divorce."
You fear it's all too soon, to my dismay;
You ask, and I consent, to stay the course.

So, we love in the shadows with a veil;
I trace the curves and arches of your lips.
Hoping time will ease this odd travail;
Savoring all that fate cannot eclipse.

You're disarming, the charming way you sleep;
My hand in yours, my soul for you to keep.

April 1, 1971

SONNET VII

Opening Day

The stadium filled with hope, the fans believe;

At last, the long-sought pennant shall be mine.

Three runs, the bases full and I perceive

The high one hard approaching from your sign.

"Beware of artful pitches, ancient knight;

The curve unwinding deftly with deceit.

You sign the pitch up high and to the right

When you know it drops sharply at my feet.

"Are you humbled your prophecy was wrong?

My endless love returned at fate's decree.

Stand back, this pitch is mine, the hit is long.

Four runs you may now add to my last three."

"Stride cautiously my friend, your path is cursed;

Take heed; it's but the bottom of the first." [9]

April 18, 1971

SONNET VIII

Linda's Sonnet

"What is the spell your words have over me?
My spirit soars, tears fall with every line.
Our storied kiss, my heart then never free;
An endless love, thereafter, yours and mine.

I sense the tumbling leaves at Roma park;
Mascara on your pillow where we sleep.
Our kisses in the shadows after dark;
Your hand secure in mine, your soul to keep.

I close my eyes and sense your pen in hand,
Each verse swept-up in dreams that dare come true.
How could I not return your love as planned?
And so, dear heart, I pledge my love to you.

I pray that in the end I am your dream;
For on this special night, it so does seem!"

May 2, 1971

SONNET IX

The Knight's Sonnet

Conflicted at the turn true love has made,

Do I counsel the apprentice to retreat?

I thought his love enchanted, a charade;

Though, now it seems that lightening does repeat.

Obsessive in his quest to reach his dream,

Persistence, nonetheless, has served him well.

His pen? A ploy to execute his scheme.

His madness; the incentive to excel.

Alas, I must admit, he loves her so!

Neither windmills nor bulls deter his quest.

Perhaps, I'll play along, that I might know

Whether he or endless love survives the test.

Ideal love is one that squares the scales;

A balance the apprentice often fails.

May 2, 1971

SONNET X

Subtle Persuasion

I revel in the passion of your kiss,
Your sentiments and comfort on display.
And yet, in sweet repose, we reminisce
How easily we can endless love misplay.

You fancy the adventure of our dreams;
Confident my faith in you is true.
Your devotion, as compelling as it seems,
Is enriched by sweet assurances from you.

We love by night, our days in search of hope
That soon our storied love will stand the test.
Our challenges, incessant; yet we cope,
For fail again and dreams arc dispossessed.

Embrace me and assure me all is right,
And together we shall dream beyond tonight.

May 12, 1971

SONNET XI

Faux Faults

We stroll the square at sunrise with resolve
To extend our endless love into the light.
Discontented in the shadows, fears evolve;
A choice that only trusting hearts incite.

You pause, look in my eyes, and ask me why
I could love you, self-centered and direct?
I revel in your passion and reply:
"Self-possession? A form of self-respect."

Just as dignity blends confidence with grace,
Assurance tempers vagary and doubt.
Your bluntness and conceit, I'll long embrace;
But pouty lips, I cannot live without.

I'll covet all these traits, your tour de force;
I choose you and your flaws without remorse.

June 20, 1971

SONNET XII

Clear Intent

Brooding storms give way to silken rain
With each adoring glance into your eyes.
Those emerald gems on starless nights refrain,
Then suddenly ignite the darkest skies.

Dawn arrives, I prevail on you to stay;
For hope shall not by night alone restore.
We walk the highland trails miles away,
Lost in love just as we were before.

"Hold me in your arms, embrace my dreams;
I take you as you are without dissent.
You think my promise less than what it seems?
Then listen as I state my clear intent:

"You are to me as dawn to endless night;
My only hope for comfort, warmth and light."

July 6, 1971

SONNET XIII

From Linda

I Much Prefer Nights to the Highlands

"Doubt not my love though words speak not my heart;

My special thoughts are always about you.

We hike the highland trails from the start,

Envisioning our endless love come true.

"Each evening as sweet darkness steals the light,

My heart I freely yield to passion's need.

All your treasured gifts are mine tonight,

Glorious night when we to love concede.

I would love you as easily in the day

As when you steal my heart by candlelight.

On morning walks you have so much to say,

While I disrupt your thoughts and words at night.

I think I'd rather kiss you in the dark,

And leave our chats for strolling in the park."

July 12, 1971

SONNET XIV

A Signature Gift and Collaboration in Rhyme.

[Poet]

You gift me the "Days of Wine and Roses," [10]

A scented kiss, idyllic and ornate.

What next from my starlet as she poses?

What more might I expect from our late date?

[Linda]

"I thought about a sweater or a card;

No; such a tasteless tribute to my love.

I draped myself in lace, so avant-garde,

A gift for you to watch me slip-out of."

[Poet]

The sheerest lace, a stunning smile, pouty lips;

Oh my, I'll take a picture; do you mind?

For no one will believe me or my scripts

As I write about the birthday gift you signed.

[Linda]

"Extravagant and funky, I concede;

But perfect for the man I love and need."

July 28, 1971

SONNET XV

The Lost Sonnet—From Linda

"We kissed; you took my breath away, then slept;

I mused about the outcome of our plan.

At light speed to the end of time, I leapt;

To trace our dream from whence it first began.

Distressed to find you wed, and I a third;

Clearly this was not as we designed.

The reasons for this outcome, dim and blurred;

Uncertain where our love was left behind.

What omen does this awkward dream reveal?

Will love and solace ever come our way?

And what if our romance is not ideal?

Will you tell me that I failed and walk away?

What is this enigma, your endless love?

Expectations I may never rise above.

September 1, 1971

SONNET XVI

Birthday Sonnet

Dawn paints the sky as Sunday morning breaks,
I'm absent without leave, alone in thought.
Your birthday nears; I'm mindful of the stakes
Should you suppose I foolishly forgot.

I surrender my case books and my lance
And muse about the woman I adore.
In honor of your birth and our romance,
I compose this verse as you turn twenty-four.

"You've blossomed so, perceptive and discreet;
A rose unfurled, so graceful and divine.
Your heart a vessel bountiful and sweet
In which my endless love and yours combine.

The day you share with Lincoln, I'll rejoice;
And pray that one day soon I'll be your choice."

January 21, 1973

SONNET XVII

For Linda's 25th Birthday

How best to touch your heart and mend our rift

When tide and time resist my every try?

Perhaps a rhyme, an everlasting gift,

Will mean more than my words alone imply.

I've failed you and love in countless ways,

Demanding more than you should rightly bear.

You see our love in many shades of grays,

While I foresee a story-book affair.

Yet when we kiss, the tones and colors merge,

A mélange of senses burst, euphoria reigns.

Distinctions that divided us converge,

The best of you and I and love remains.

I wish you love wrapped in a silver bow.

As for my love, you stole it long ago.

February 21, 1974

SONNET XVIII

My Crime

Oh love untrue, there is no scourge like thee.

My heart once pledged in trust, then tossed aside;

My dreams deprived of pride, then never free;

My crime? To let my heart in yours confide.

Defenseless to the splendor of your eyes,

You swore enduring love with solemn tears.

And then your scarlet letter, my surprise;

Our endless love is not as it appears.

You warned me, your love has no fair rule;

I must presume 'til love or truth emerge.'

With faith in you, you played me like a fool

Just long enough to see our lives diverge.

I've earned my fate; your love and its despair.

And yes, it's true, that all in love is fair.

February 6, 1975

SONNET XIX

Misimpressions[11]

A fool for love, as if no tax is due

For faith and honor lost in your pursuit.

"This Love," you said a thousand times, "is true."

And yet that which is truth your acts dispute.

One star-filled night in March, decades ago,

You merged your heart with mine; my finest day.

We fell in love, implausibly, I know;

And yet through storms and doubt love found its way.

How could it be, a love that knew no bounds

Slipped through my hands like simple grains of sand?

Your dreams stream still, your wistfulness resounds;

Then fell your tears; pearls cast at your command.

I've wondered all these years, was your love true?

Or did I your intentions misconstrue?

April 17, 2020

SONNET XX

Intercession of the Sonnets

Your kiss in sweet repose, a promise past

As star-crossed love is lost in folds of time.

Our storied love, to sorrow, swiftly cast;

Discarded and consigned to prose and rhyme.

Then, sonnets rise; hope surges from the dust.

The poet's pen assigns old love as new.

Imagery shapes destiny and trust;

Spirits merge and fantasies come true.

Sweeter still, your candidness assures

Our broken hearts will mend despite my fears.

Worn doubts dare not intrude, for love endures;

And hope returns in doting cycs and tears.

Heartened by your longing as we kiss,

The sonnets our forsaken dreams dismiss.

April 7, 2020

SONNET XXI

Let Time Not Judge

Let time not judge the splendor of your smile,
Time passage has no privilege over you.
A glance, my heart then lost, as was your style;
Sensations, myths and rhymes of dreams come true.

"The warmth and fervor of your lips have past,"
Says time, the thief whose gifts do not repeat.
"Your dreams have set; they shall not be recast."
Let time not judge your smile with such conceit.

For were there not rare moments in our lives
When hope brought joy and comfort to our hearts?
The image of your smile, our love arrives;
What better proof that dreams and truth are parts?

Let time not judge the splendor of your smile;
Let myth, lore and fantasy stand trial.

April 24, 2020

SONNET XXII

The Ill-Considered Choices of My Youth

Too late, this modest verse, to make amends
For the ill-considered choices of my youth.
Bewildered by the sorcery love attends,
I could not, to your face, confess the truth.

You asked me what my feelings were for you,
What expectations I might entertain.
I spoke in riddles, blurring what was true,
Carefully phrased to spare you any pain.

How could I say I loved another more,
As you nestled in my arms in sweet repose?
I treasured you, a fact to which I swore,
Words truer still than you would e'er suppose.

There were some truths that I could never speak,
Lest anguished hearts and other havoc wreak.

August 30, 2020

SONNET XXIII

A Debt Long Due My Father

In silent thought my father comes to mind,
A peaceful spirit, principled and bold.
Ninety-nine this day, had fate been so inclined;
Modest, heroic, his legend widely told.

"Soon comes a day you have to be a man,"
He counseled me, lest forethought be misspent.
Then, not another lecture, word, or plan;
He proved by his own measure what he meant.

Respect for all, an elemental creed,
That which he sowed was countless times returned.
His dreams deferred to not their cost exceed,
And quarrels solved without his bridges burned.

My father was the greatest man I knew.
My debt for lessons learned, long overdue.

November 23, 2020

SONNET XXIV

My Mother Speaks in Rhymes

My mother was a force, though calming soul.
She taught me how to dream and led the way.
"Without a dream, one cannot reach her goal,"
Countless times I heard my mother say.

She's right, of course, as mothers always are.
Her goals were shaped to make my dreams come true.
Throughout my life she lit the guiding star
As I set off to destiny pursue.

She never knew a stranger nor a foe.
Friends were family, as honored as her own.
She preached the golden rule for all to know,
That we for last impressions must atone.

My mother spoke in verses, prose and rhymes
On how to sort the best and worst of times.

December 24, 2020

SONNET XXV

Long Endure the Treasured Times—
Allusions from a Poet's Pen

My thoughts at peace I turn to moments fine,
Those fleeting joys for which we hoped and dreamed.
The best of these, my heart and yours align;
Our expectations soon to be redeemed.

Alas, true love befell us at an age
When youth and inexperience foiled the plan.
With neither poise nor prudence at that stage,
Our dreams to dust transformed as they began.

Deprived of hope, I had but one last thought;
Post every verse to you I ever wrote.
A scheme like this, unwise, with danger fraught.
I held my breath dispatching every note.

I prayed our storied love would long endure;
A dream the poet's pen does now assure.

August 14, 2023

SONNET XXVI
Stumbling in Our Youth

When I too soon surrendered to your smile,
Ordained were we to share a hopeless dream.
Bind my heart with yours through wit or guile,
With endless love the prize, or it did seem.

I wonder now, too old to reason why
Our love could not ascend to the ideal.
A step too far, the truth a peak too high;
Where lay the fatal flaw in our ordeal?

Inclined was I to dream beyond my reach;
Erratic, your commitment to accede.
A wistful kiss, a verse, a stirring speech,
Insufficient to satisfy your need.

Unwittingly, we stumbled in our youth,
Confusing our illusions for the truth!

September 16, 2023

SONNET XXVII

While Glory Reigns

No shelter, save the dawn, from ruthless time;
Relentless in devouring mind and soul.
Where lost our special moments so sublime?
Where lie the parts of loving hearts once whole?

The years pass rapt in thought, lost in review.
From dreams to just rewards I muse and reap.
What if this choice I pass or that pursue?
What if I stop and think before I leap?

Who knows what might have been had we deferred
The choices made when you and I were young?
Resolving might-have-beens, a bit absurd!
How quickly might the pendulum have swung?

It's late, let's love, exploit what time remains;
Accept our choices made while glory reigns.

September 16, 2023

SONNET XXVIII

Just Us Two

How grand was love when it was just us two?

No children, courts or clients to indulge.

To kiss, embrace, a joy; our hearts renew.

No tears or fears or failings to divulge.

Children were our wish in god's grand scheme;

The Law, a jealous mistress not ignored.

What choice had we to share our life-long dream?

I take you, you take me, a just accord.

The children raised with honor and resolve;

You led them to discernment by the hand.

My windmills slain, too soon did we evolve

To live as one, apart, at fate's command?

For forty-seven years we shared a dream;

Just us two, or so it once did seem.

September 23, 2023

SONNET XXIX

Always Sentimental About You

How strange to grow this old and feel so young.

It happens when I'm mindful of the past.

To others we belonged, our song unsung;

And yet we knew that dance was not our last.

Years later misadventure brought me back

To that moment I first set my eyes on you.

A kiss and all that was faded to black.

And what remained? Our endless love come-true.

Was it your eyes or smile that won my heart?

You say, "our love was simply meant to be."

I challenge that, fate played a lesser part;

'Twas you who stole my love away from me!

I wonder why of all the dreams I knew,

I'm always sentimental about you?

September 25, 2023

SONNET XXX

Presence

To steer you from the law was by design;
Too hostile to consume another soul.
You made your way as wit and guile align,
When poise and presence merged and made you whole.

Three children on your own test your resolve;
Your mother always there to lend a hand.
The best schools, your support and they evolve.
As once did you, they've learned to take a stand.

"Choose roads that I did not," I once advised;
There's much to learn from paths that post no signs.
You've done precisely that; I'm not surprised
For one who leaps and paints outside the lines.

A father to his son, the chain endures.
Like my father, I've found my dreams in yours.

September 27, 2023

SONNET XXXI

Starlight

Beyond a father's dream your life unfolds,
Like petals of a stylish crimson rose.
With pride and strength of will your spirit molds.
As hope renews your dreams, composure grows.

Determined to succeed all on your own,
You roam from one adventure to the next.
When time demands you choose a path unknown,
And still you meet your goals in all respects.

One day as if by fate two dreams appear;
Son and daughter, atonement long past due.
Love fills your heart; your doubts and worries clear,
For now the world contends with three of you.

I once foretold you'd be the brightest star.
I search the darkest skies and find you are!

October 11, 2023

SONNET XXXII

And What is Gold Remains

When to the force of time the light recedes,
Your brunette strands to grey, your smile to tears;
Yet even then, as gloom to love concedes,
I'll be there at your side to ease your fears.

Love does not thrive in joy and fade in grief,
An endless love endures despite the cost.
Till death we vowed, for that is our belief;
And what is gold remains, rejecting Frost.

It's been a ride, this journey we two share,
Through joys and sorrows past, hope yet exists.
Though not ideal, our partnership is fair,
And that, dear heart, is why our love persists.

It always seemed ideal love was best.
Perhaps, I should have focused on the rest.

October 29, 2023

SONNET XXXIII

Shared Sensibilities

In wistful thought we sort our moments past,
Forty-seven years of values learned.
Through quarrels, tears, a few aspersions cast,
Not a rail of our bridges have we burned.

More diverse than alike, our minds and hearts;
Distinction, the appeal that draws us near.
Learning to forgive by fits and starts,
Resolving to forget; perhaps, next year.

We brace our love with trust and shared respect,
Preferring to console than to be right.
I glance into your eyes and we connect,
Without a word to startle or incite.

I knew the day we met you were ideal.
Just how much so will time and tide reveal.

March 1, 2024

SONNET XXXIV

Nostalgia—Never Late

I strive to hold my thoughts of thee as dear
As when the stars first graced me with your heart.
The fog of decades past, illusions clear;
What solace might this sonnet now impart?

Nostalgia, like a star-filled sky retreats
Into darkness, an abyss in time and space.
'Tis here, a stage, where fantasy repeats
And endless love is lost without a trace.

This script neglects the splendor of your kiss;
Those sky-blue eyes; a heart that seldom speaks.
Discarded is your pledge, so near a miss;
And tears like pearls that fall from blushing cheeks.

Nostalgia, that enticing, sorcerous state
Where fantasy and lore are never late.

March 12, 2024

SONNET XXXV

And Nothing More

The morning star drifts northward toward due east
Foreshadowing the season we two met.
Our youth in bloom, my hopes, your whims released;
Remembrances to savor, not forget.

And to this end, so many verses penned,
I best recall a lavish kiss from you.
Though wondrous dreams your lush, sweet lips transcend,
Your kiss did not my fantasies make true.

Misgivings to resolve? A few remain.
Should fate, the instant we two met, restore,
What outcome then, with hindsight's sweet refrain,
"A kiss is just a kiss and nothing more?"

What is this wistful day that haunts the past?
The advent of a love I sha'nt outlast.

March 16, 2024

SONNET XXXVI

Intimation

The poet pens a sonnet steeped in lore,
An adaptation fate would not decree.
"What curse or havoc would my pen implore
Should providence return her love to me?"

Preferring not to dwell on choices past,
He scribes the curves and arches of her lips.
Her splendor and magnificence recast,
The sonnet spares what fate could not eclipse.

The subtle intimation of a smile
Returns the poet's heart to moments fine.
Though love was lost through lack of wit and wile,
Perception and reality align.

The poet pens a sonnet steeped in lore,
The outcome? Slightly better than before.

March 31, 2024

SONNET XXXVII

John Keats and Fanny Brawne; What if?

I read in awe a tale of true romance,

The letters Keats once wrote to Fanny Brawne.[12]

Can love so tax the mind and heart, by chance,

To leave young Keats defeated and withdrawn?

To claim that he would die for love, for her,

Ravished by a need he won't resist;[13]

To reason against reason, to defer;

The pain too great to obviate the tryst.[14]

Near death, a final plea, his frame a wraith,

Thankful that the grave shall see him rest.[15]

Longing for her arms, a pledge of faith,

Or else struck down with lightning by request.[16]

Would such a love have thrived, profound and true,

Had health not failed and luring youth ensue?

April 2, 2024

SONNET XXXVIII

From This Universe to the Next

In pensive thought I reach the great divide,

A portal at the edge of time and space.

Where wit and intuition were my guide,

A step and both are lost without a trace.

Who is this man, devoid of self and sense;

Reconceived in a cosmos of blue stars?

Where is this place; familiar, yet intense?

Who is this love who speaks of hers and ours?

Twin stars ignite the shadows in the skies,

With twice the hope and promise for each day.

Whose thoughts are these, original and wise?

Whose voice is this with so much yet to say?

Transition is god's way to square the scales.

Begin anew till empathy prevails.

April 3, 2024

SONNET XXXIX

La Conquistadora Chapel—1957

For my Grandmother

A first-born son, the duty fell to me
To walk my aging grandmother to mass.
"The second pew, the middle seat," said she;
I sat and spied the cross, the sainted glass.

Gram long preferred this chapel off the side,
The hand-carved saint perched stately in her niche.
"She walked here with your ancestors astride;
Bow your head, say a prayer, I don't care which."

My visits now are fleeting and discreet,
This chapel that my grandmother adored.
I see through tears the pew, the middle seat
And all the saints and symbols she implored.

"I walk through time, the moments we once knew
And pray the sainted virgin walks with you."

April 4, 2024

SONNET XL

Words and Deeds

Our love is too inconstant to be true;
Each week a tiff or tantrum to redress.
No sooner do we cross the line we drew,
Tears fall like pearls; we yield and reassess.

And so it goes, as it has gone for years;
We pledge our hearts but will not cede our souls.
We dance around our fits to ease our fears,
Yet manage to fulfill our dreams and goals.

It's not about the sentiments we feel;
Enduring love is forged by words and deeds.
You keep your soul; I pose a better deal;
Let honesty and candor serve our needs.

We fret about our feelings; not our trust.
It's time that we speak freely and adjust.

April 9, 2024

NOTES

1. poetryfoundation.org/articles/70051/learning-the-sonnet.

2. poetryfoundation.org/learn/glossary-terms/shakespearean-sonnet.

3. Jaramillo, Arturo Lewis, *Conversations with Quijóte, A Poet's Decades-Long Quest to Reconcile His Ideal Love Affair with Reality,* Sunstone Press (2019); Jaramillo, Arturo L., *Impressions Through a Timeworn Lens, an Anthology of Poetry,* Sunstone Press (2024).

4. Jaramillo, A.L. (2019) *A Preface to my Poetry,* p. 86.

5. Jaramillo, A.L. (2024) *Introduction.*

6. Sonnets I through XVIII, were initially published in Jaramillo, Arturo Lewis, *Conversations with Quijóte, A Poet's Decades-Long Quest to Reconcile His Ideal Love Affair with Reality,* Sunstone Press (2019).

7. Frost, Robert, *Nothing Gold Can* Stay (1923).

8. Jaramillo, A. L., *Conversations with Quijóte a poet's decades-long quest to reconcile his ideal love affair with reality* (Sunstone Press, 2019), *Foreword,* p. 41 (Quijóte is the famous knight created by Miguel de Cervantes Saavedra in his famous novel, *Don Quijote De La Mancha* (1605). Quijóte was to thc author of this book a contemporary folk hero in the late nineteen sixties. Given Quijóte's legendary knowledge of the art of chivalry, his remarkable insight, empathy and benevolence, the author imagined Quijóte as his mentor, muse and alter ego. That notion continues even today).

9. In matters of love and romance, Quijóte was quick to offer advice to the author of this

book, even applying the strategy and situations in a baseball game as part of his guidance when necessary to make a point. See Jaramillo, A. L. (2019) *Analyzing the Curve with Quijóte*, p. 202-204.

10. Henry Mancini and Johnny Mercer, *Days of Wine and Roses*, a song from the film of the same name (1962).

11. Sonnets XIX through XXXII, were initially published in Jaramillo, Arturo L., *Impressions Through a Timeworn Lens, an Anthology of Poetry,* Sunstone Press (2024).

12. Keats, John, *Bright Star: Love Letters and Poems of John Keats to Fanny Brawne,* Penguin Books (2009).

13. Keats, J (2009) *Letter VIII*, 13 October (1819).

14. Keats, J (2009) *Letter VIII*, 13 October (1819).

15. Keats, J (2009) *Letter XXXVII* (1821).

16. Keats, J (2009) *Letter XXXVII* (1821).

Printed in the USA
CPSIA information can be obtained
at www.ICGtesting.com
CBHW081716080824
12784CB00049B/532